The Organ Music of
ALEXANDRE GUILMANT

Book One

A Performing Edition by
Malcolm Archer

Kevin Mayhew

We hope you enjoy *The Organ Music of Alexandre Guilmant* Book 1.
A further collection is available from your local music or Christian bookshop.

In case of difficulty, please contact the publisher
direct by writing to:

The Sales Department
KEVIN MAYHEW LTD
Rattlesden
Bury St Edmunds
Suffolk IP30 0SZ

Phone 0449 737978
Fax 0449 737834

Please ask for our complete catalogue of outstanding Church Music.

Front Cover: *The Ascension* by William Blake (1757-1827).
The Fitzwilliam Museum, Cambridge.
Photograph: © Woodmansterne Picture Library.
Reproduced by kind permission.

First published in Great Britain in 1992 by
KEVIN MAYHEW LTD
Rattlesden
Bury St Edmunds
Suffolk IP30 0SZ

© Copyright 1992 by Kevin Mayhew Ltd

ISBN 0 86209 298 1

Cover design by Graham Johnstone

Printed and bound in Great Britain

Contents

Foreword

Alexandre Guilmant (1837-1911) was born in Boulogne-sur-Mer, France. He came from a family of organists and organ builders and though he studied briefly with the famous Belgium organist and composer Jaak Nikolaas Lemmens, he was mainly self-taught.

For many years he was organist of the Trinité, Paris, and had an outstanding career as a recitalist, especially as an exponent of the Cavaillé-Coll organ, with its unsurpassed quality and tonal range. He travelled throughout Europe and the USA, playing to enthusiastic audiences.

He was much in demand as a teacher and, as successor to Widor at the Conservatoire, his pupils included Joseph Bonnet and Marcel Dupré.

Guilmant's compositional output, mostly for organ or voices, is large. Much of his registration was for the distinctive Cavaillé-Coll sound which is not available to most organists outside France. Thus, in this performing edition of some of his most approachable music I have suggested a layout which takes this into account.

I have also endeavoured to clear away the kind of editorial encrustations which result in the actual notes fighting to peep through the gaps in the instructions. In this edition the notes are left to speak for themselves so that the page is clear and uncluttered: something of which I believe Guilmant – himself a proponent of simplicity, clean phrasing and impeccable technique – would have approved.

MALCOLM ARCHER

VERSET

Alexandre Guilmant

Allegro moderato (♩ = 92)

MINUET

Alexandre Guilmant

INVOCATION in E♭

Alexandre Guilmant

– Gt. to Ped.

espressivo

Sw. *p*

BERCEUSE

based on a French Noël

Alexandre Guilmant

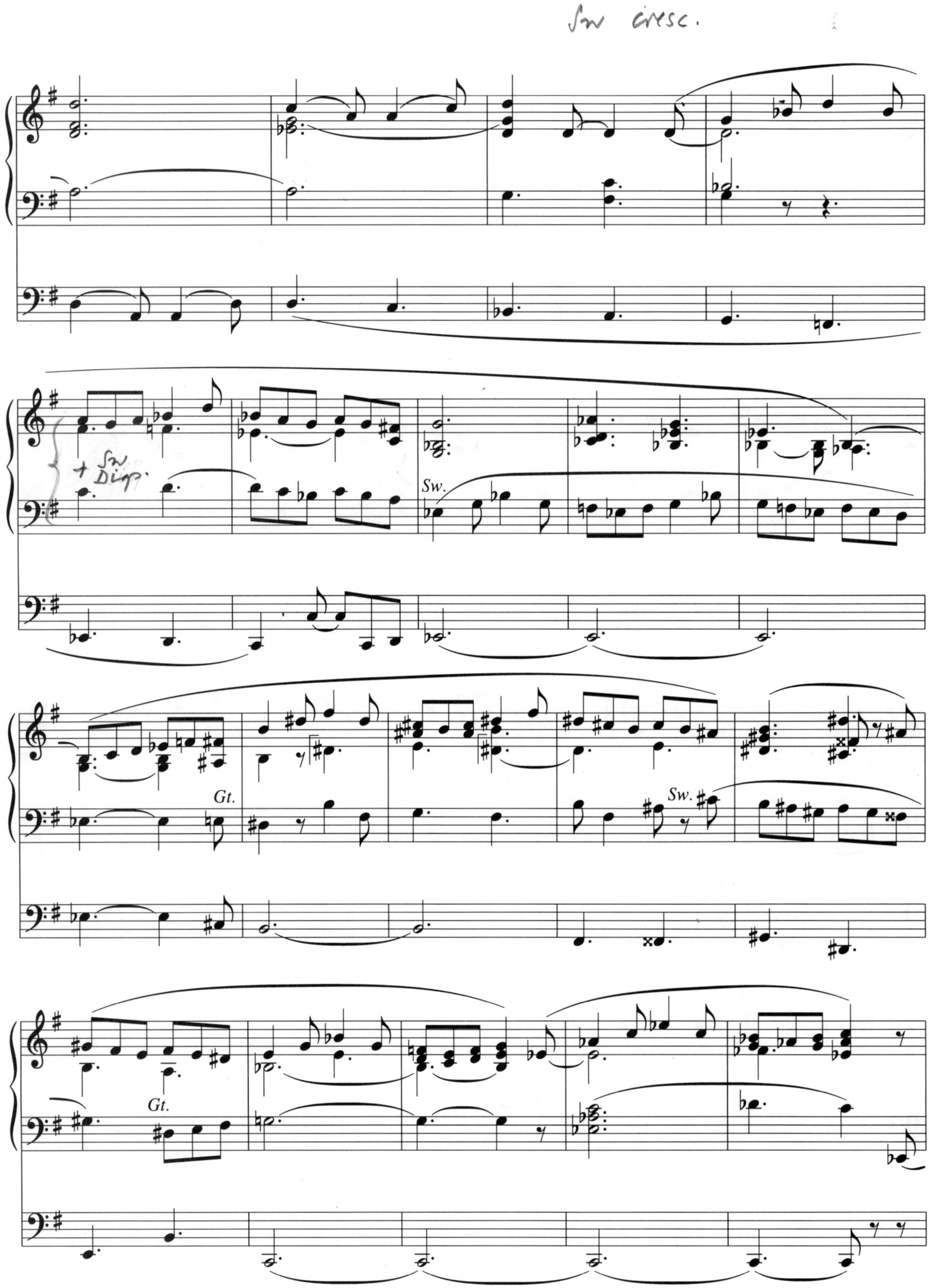
Sw cresc.
+ Sw Diap.
Sw.
Gt.
Sw.
Gt.

MELODY

Alexandre Guilmant

Andante cantabile (♩ = 96)

+ pedal couplers

L.H.

COMMUNION in G

Alexandre Guilmant

29

PRAYER II

Alexandre Guilmant

32

OFFERTORY in G

Alexandre Guilmant

+ Gt. to Ped.

MEDITATION in B minor

Alexandre Guilmant

Andante quasi adagio (♩ = 50)

PASTORALE

Alexandre Guilmant

49

MARCH in D

Alexandre Guilmant

53

56

ELEVATION

Alexandre Guilmant